THE FUTURE OF HIGHER EDUCATION

How Emerging Technologies Will Change Education Forever

By Lasse Rouhiainen

www.lasserouhiainen.com

ISBN-3:978-1539450139

ISBN-10:1539450139

ALSO FROM LASSE ROUHIAINEN

101 Facebook Marketing Tips and Strategies for Small Businesses

101 Video Marketing Tips and Strategies for Small Businesses

Smart Social Media: Your Guide to Becoming a Highly Paid Social Media Manager

TABLE OF CONTENT

INTRODUCTION

"Education is the most powerful weapon which you can use to change the world."

- Nelson Mandela

Do you believe that traditional education could be improved with the development of new technologies?

Are you interested in learning the best practices of running a successful and effective online course?

Have you ever thought about the potential impact that artificial intelligence could have on classrooms around the world?

Since 2007, I have offered online learning opportunities in three different languages to students across more than 40 countries. I have made many mistakes, but also learned a lot of valuable lessons over the years. I have a passion for education in general, coupled with a deep interest in the development of new technologies, including artificial intelligence, virtual reality, and the applications and opportunities afforded by these innovations for the near future.

As I searched for books that thoughtfully examine the applications of future technologies to education, I was not able to find a lot of material, which inspired me to write my own. In today's world, changes in technology are happening much faster than we can appreciate, and we have a unique opportunity to learn from and apply these tools in new and creative ways, impacting the ways that we learn every day.

This book is not meant to be a profound academic research paper, filled with complicated charts and terms, but rather a short guide for those who are interested in the future of education as it relates to technology. The material is to the point and practical, offering quick bullet points and helpful recommendations for educators. You'll also find short summaries of the most important developments and applications in technology, which are designed to awaken your own sense of curiosity.

While I have not covered every aspect of technology and education comprehensively, I hope that you will see my own fascination with this topic and be inspired to consider the world of possibilities opening up for educators through new technologies.

Chapter 1 introduces the best practices and techniques for e-learning that I have picked up over the years and wanted to share with others. The realm of online learning is experiencing incredible growth. Although this book is mainly targeted toward university-level educators, the tips and practices covered in this chapter can be applied by any online instructor, including those developing and selling their own courses online.

While there are a number of topics in this book, I have the most experience in the field of e-learning. I have intentionally excluded the history of the e-learning market and its growth, choosing instead to provide more practical applications and easy-to-follow steps that educators can use in their own courses.

Chapter 2 shares how artificial intelligence will impact our world in the not-so-distant future. Here, you'll find some key ideas about the ways in which both students and teachers will benefit as artificial intelligence is used in online classrooms. Out of all of the emerging technologies, I believe that AI is the one with the greatest potential for impact on the world of education, as well as for society as a whole. I highly recommend studying this area more deeply and considering the ways that you can implement and embrace the opportunities generated by this technology.

Chapter 3 shares some of the cases in which virtual reality and augmented reality can and have been implemented in education, providing examples of the ways that these immersive technologies can be applied. While both offer unique ways to enhance the excitement and motivation of students, they need to be implemented correctly in order to avoid the potential pitfalls associated with each.

Chapter 4 shares a brief picture of the skills that will be most sought after in the world of the future, especially when considering the effects of the technologies that we've discussed. While there are numerous skills that will be vital in the new job markets, I've included a list of 24 skills that I believe are the most important to acquire and improve, helping people to live and work in a way that is harmonious with new technical developments.

Because this is a particularly large topic, I have also included some valuable opinions on the world of technology and education from various experts in their fields. These experts include:

- Ulla Engeström - Founder and CEO of ThingLink Interactive
- Topi Litmanen - Chief Educational Scientist, Ph.D., Claned.com
- Pasi Tuominen - Customer Experience Professional, Educator and Lecturer at HAAGA-HELIA University of Applied Sciences
- Satu Järvinen - Director of Education Services at Koulu Group

Each of these experts will provide some short but insightful viewpoints regarding the applications of the emergent technologies.

I wish you an enjoyable reading experience as you delve into this brief introduction of the emerging technologies and the ways in which they will change the face of education. I hope that you are inspired to embrace new ideas and questions, recognizing the value of each as they are developed, and implementing them in innovative ways for you.

CHAPTER 1

E-Learning and Online Learning Best Practices

"E-Learning doesn't just "happen"! It requires careful planning and implementation."

- Anonymous

Would you like to conduct effective and engaging online courses? Whether you've ever led virtual classes in the past or are just getting started in the world of online learning, this chapter will give you a lot of practical information that can help you to improve your teaching techniques.

In most circles, the term "e-learning" refers to a course delivered on the Internet using an online learning management system (LMS), rather than providing traditional instruction in a classroom setting in which students and teachers are physically in the same space. The term "blended learning" refers to a mixture of online learning with face-to-face classes and seems to offer the best student outcomes due to the additional human elements afforded to both students and teachers. When you are first beginning to use e-learning tools, it is recommended that you use blended learning, to help you understand the differences between virtual and physical teaching methods and how each should be employed.

The term "MOOC" means a massive open online course. This concept became very popular in 2012, when several universities in the United States started testing them on their campuses. However, the largest drawback to this kind of learning environment is that the dropout rates tend to be very high. Therefore, if you are just beginning to teach online courses, I recommend starting with fewer students, gaining experience, before moving on to MOOCs.

Figure 1.1. E-learning.

E-learning is a very broad topic. While there is a lot of information that can help you to be more successful as a virtual teacher, the tips below have been compiled from my personal experience in facilitating online courses over the past decade. While they are not comprehensive, they can help you to get going in the right direction. The following are 14 best practices on how you can effectively run e-learning courses.

1. Make Sure the Content is Accessible With a Mobile Phone

As you design your online course, make sure to account for mobile access, as recent trends have shown that students are likely to view content from their smartphones or tablets. This allows students to learn while on the go, which is one of the things that online students are looking for. It also affords a unique opportunity for students to make the most of their down time, perhaps a long bus ride or a lunch break at work, decreasing the dropout rate for a course.

Check all of your content to make sure that videos play back on various mobile devices, including Android and iOS operating systems, and are easy to watch while they are being played. Consider how any text shown may look from a small screen. Vertical video composition can also make it easier for students to take advantage of their mobile devices for playback of lectures or content.

2. Use Video as Your Main Form of Content

More than ever before, online students are seeking out video content. Video is not just something that they enjoy, but is also something that surrounds them all the time, whether it is for social interaction through Snapchat or Facebook, learning about something new through a YouTube tutorial, or simply sitting back and watching television.

Figure 1.2. Online Video Education.

In terms of online learning, video is one of the most powerful tools at your disposal. Here are just a few of the benefits offered through video:

- Video content can be more interesting and directly relevant to students than text.

- Video is easy to review more than once, allowing students to watch parts of the content repeatedly, as needed.

- Video can be accessed from mobile devices and tablets when set up correctly by the facilitator.

- Video content is often more memorable than text.

- Last, but not least, video content can catch the attention of students who are living in a world of distraction, engaging their senses more effectively than traditional text.

As you implement video content in your online courses, here are some of the action steps you can take to maximize the effectiveness of your content:

- **Keep videos short and to the point.** On average, your videos should run between 5 and 6 minutes in length. Studies have shown that students tend to lose interest or become distracted during longer video sessions. If you are covering an expansive topic, consider breaking things up into a series of focused videos, which will then make it easier for your students to review as needed.

- At the end of each video, **include a question** that drives your students to do their own research or try out a new skill related to the content of the video.

- Invest in good recording equipment and make sure that any background noise is addressed, as poor audio quality can distract your students from your message.

- Along with good recording equipment, make sure to **pace your videos well,** using intonation and enunciation to make your messages easy to understand and engaging, while speaking roughly 10-15% faster than in daily conversation so that topics do not drag on.

- When possible, try to **record multiple videos in a single session**. This can help you to develop rhythms in your content and to manage your time as an instructor well.

- Within the video itself, seek out opportunities to **create movement within the content**. If you are screen sharing, don't leave your screen in the same place for extended periods of time. Use engaging colors and professional design on all media.

- Consider using a **combination of tools within your video,** sharing information through PowerPoint, a view of your browser, relevant sites, and videos of you as the instructor.

- **Host your videos professionally using services like Vimeo Pro,** rather than depending on YouTube.

- **Add secondary materials** to your course for students to review, including handouts or instructional challenges in which the students can apply their knowledge of a new tool in a hands-on way.

- **Invite your students to openly share their feedback** and adapt your teaching style accordingly.

3. Harness the Power of Student Feedback

One of the hallmarks of a great online instructor is that they listen to and learn from student feedback. This is one of the key tools in a teacher's arsenal in order to improve content effectively.

When you are first getting started as an online instructor, you may want to ask for student feedback at the completion of each new module or section. Things that you might want to ask are: Which tools helped you to learn the best in this section? Was anything unclear? What did you enjoy most about this section?

It is also helpful to give your students multiple ways to communicate their feedback to you. While the forum can be a great tool for reaching the most active students, you may need to get a little bit more creative to reach the rest of your students so that you can get well-rounded feedback. While the most active 20% of your class is important, it can also be helpful to find out why your inactive students have not engaged in the class.

Sending out an email or an anonymous survey through Google Docs can help you to do this, or you may want to reach out in a new way and ask for students to send a feedback video using a tool like Screencastify (_www.screencastify.com_) or a Cloud App _(www.getcloudapp.com)_, which allows students to create 15-second videos.

As you seek out feedback, remember to keep your questions open-ended, asking general and specific questions, such as: How would you improve this content? Which activities or resources were the most helpful to you? Which ones were the least helpful?

As a whole, student feedback is the fastest and best way to improve the experiences your students have while in your class, increasing your chances of making a long-term impact with your content.

4. Drip-Feeding Your Content

In some cases, students enroll in courses with full access to all course content. As they try to maneuver their way through the materials on their own, they can get confused, which can lead them to become unmotivated.

Drip-feeding is a common practice in which instructors schedule the content delivery for lessons or modules. Instead of having full access to all the course materials at once, students have access to new lesson materials in scheduled segments.

There are numerous benefits associated with content being drip-fed to students. This method provides greater clarity and structure to the students, helping them to focus on what is most relevant and important, which can keep their motivation levels up. It also makes it easier for the instructor to facilitate the course, as each week brings a new topic.

For those wanting more control over their delivery methods, many content delivery systems offer settings that will not allow students to access the next module before they have completed their quizzes or assignments in the previous one.

5. Take Time to Learn About Your Learning Platform

There are a number of great learning platforms on the market today, including Moodle, Blackboard, Canvas, Claned, and many others. Most of these platforms offer great tutorial videos to help new users become accustomed to the tools and features provided. Take advantage of these tools to maximize your online course.

While platform videos can be helpful, instructors can also reach out to other facilitators using the tool to find out about the creative ways in which the platform can be used. Consider speaking with other teachers in your organization or spending some time researching best practices for the platform online.

As you learn about the power of your platform, make sure that you explore the analytics features. These tools provide metrics like how many students have visited the course, how they are engaging with the content, and how long students are spending in particular sections of the module. This can help you to spot trends in student engagement, which you can then use to improve your course.

6. Communicate Effectively Through Email

While there are a number of ways to communicate with your students, email is still the most important tool at your disposal. For most students, this is the #1 way that they will expect communication, including reminders and basic information.

At a minimum, instructors should plan to send out a weekly email at the start of each module, providing clear instructions about any assignments or tools that will be introduced or due that week. Along with factual information, teachers can help their students to connect with their courses by sending interesting articles, tips, or other sources of inspiration to excite the students and encourage engagement.

Figure 1.3. Email Marketing.

Another way to use email to increase student engagement is to review the metrics from your platform to check in on the students who have not visited the course within the past 5-7 days and send them an email reminder. I picked up this tip from Aki Taanila at Haaga-Helia University of Applied Sciences, and it is a great way to encourage inactive students to re-engage in the course.

In your reminder email, mention that you noticed that they hadn't been to the course in a while and ask them if they have any questions. Within your email, encourage them to respond to the email if they still plan to continue on with the course. This gives students an action step to respond to, which can help them start to participate more actively.

Last, but not least, email can be used to send interesting or surprising information about the topic covered in that week's module. A good time for this kind of email is at the end of the week, as it provides students with a chance to review what they've learned and discover ways that others are applying the information covered.

7. Email Automation in e-Learning

When you design an online curriculum, automated email communication can be a valuable tool, especially if you plan to teach on a topic more than once. Not every email communication can be automated, especially when dealing with specific student questions, but in general, automation can save you time and energy as an instructor.

Implementing email automation for the first time in a course requires some input from people who are familiar with the benefits and obstacles associated with this particular technology. In order to bring email automation into your course, consider looking into the ways that it is used in other sectors, as well as the ways that other instructors in your field may be using it.

Every time you create a course, you can create a set of pre-written emails that will motivate and guide students. These emails can be scheduled to be sent at particular dates and times throughout the course.

Depending on the course you are teaching, you may want to consider creating some of these kinds of correspondence in advance to be sent out automatically:

- Welcome email with basic instructions on how to get started in the class;
- Weekly emails sent on the same day each week with motivational content and information about that week's topics;
- Reminder emails about major assignments or for students who may be missing course requirements;
- FAQs for important assignments and/or exams.

Remember to divide your pre-written content into short, easy-to-read segments in order to keep the attention of your students.

Many of the email marketing tools offer an array of automations, including options for students to respond to a quick multiple choice question, such as a question about whether or not that student understands a particular tool or assignment, and then to save those results for the instructor to review. This provides students with an opportunity to give meaningful feedback with a quick touch of a button. The system can then send out an email based on the response given, in this case, perhaps including additional resources for the student, which allows the instructor to interact with students in a more personalized, yet efficient, manner.

Because of the power and complexity of some of these automations, it is helpful to spend some time with an email automation specialist when you first begin to use this kind of technology.

In the future, artificial intelligence will help to create these kinds of automations, providing even more powerful systems.

8. Create Clear Instructions to Avoid Student Confusion

In many cases, students get started in a course without fully understanding the instructor's expectations for their involvement in the course. To avoid this issue and set up your students for success, it is important to clearly communicate your expectations for the course, learning activities, and student objectives. This can include things like what resources are available and how to use them, as well as what kinds of learning modalities the students will use in the course, such as visual or auditory content.

Focus your energy on the beginning of the course, which usually requires the most attention from your students. Helping them to start off well can set the pace for how your students will interact during the remainder of the course.

As you communicate these things, be sure to sell the "why" of the course. This may sometimes be called the learning outcomes. It serves to explain how the students will be able to apply what they're learning to their lives, either directly or indirectly. When possible, try to give at least two "whys," one for students who are just starting to explore the topic and one for students who are delving deeper into a topic they are already somewhat familiar with.

Establish timetables and due dates, but include some flexibility so that students can catch up if they fall behind. Most students enrolled in online courses seek out these kinds of classes because of the flexibility they offer.

Create a video to welcome students to the course, showing your face when possible to encourage personal connection. Share any first steps the students should take to familiarize themselves with the course content. It can also be helpful to talk about the course schedule and how the students can expect to have access to you through the message board, email, or other avenues.

Finally, create an FAQ document with at least 8-10 questions for the students so that they can easily access this information as needed. Encourage the students to print out a copy of this document for easy access. Included in your FAQ should be general questions about things like how much time they should expect to spend on readings or lectures each week, as well as technical questions like how to troubleshoot for video playback issues. Add to this document throughout the course as you receive and review student feedback.

9. Utilize Forums and Quizzes Effectively

For an online course, the forum is often the heart of all course activity. You can know that you have a successful course when you observe a lot of student engagement within the forum. Likewise, a lack of engagement in the forum usually indicates a lack of engagement with students.

The forum should be a place that gets students excited about the course topics and inspires them to apply what they are learning. As you post to the forum personally, remember to communicate in a way that resonates with your students.

Model what kinds of interactions you want to see on the forum by sharing success stories, case studies, questions to ponder, and current events. Encourage your students to reflect and respond to these on the forum, going deeper than a simple opinion as they articulate their thoughts.

Figure 1.4. Online Forums.

You can also encourage students to post their own discussions around current events and topics, sharing how various links and events relate to the information in the course. Urge your students to upload a picture of themselves to their student profile, which can also help to personalize their content.

It is possible to create and use Facebook groups to encourage discussions as well, but recognize that it can be more difficult to have threaded conversations outside of the learning platform.

You can also invite students to review what they've learned through quizzes at the end of every module or section. This is a great way to allow students to self-check their understanding of a topic. Generally, multiple choice questions are the most helpful, as you can set up your quiz in a way that allows students to see the correct answers and their total score at the end of a quiz. Open-ended questions with specific instructions can also help you to monitor how well your students grasp the topic at hand.

10. Measure Student Engagement and Activity Levels

In the past few years, technology has evolved in such a way that it has opened up new measurement tools that can allow greater insights into trends and metrics than ever before. This is true in every field of business, but is truly vital to success in the e-learning market.

Every online instructor should take the time to learn about the analytics tools offered by their learning platform. While this can seem like a daunting task, it will pay off in the long run, as it will help teachers to better understand how their students interact with content, allowing them to make changes in their courses, adapting them as needed to make them as engaging and effective as possible.

Here are some of the most important course metrics you can analyze as an online instructor:

- **Percentage of active users on a weekly basis:** This can be particularly helpful when comparing different cycles of the same class, to see if various changes in the course lead to more activity from students.

- **Most popular content:** By seeing which content is viewed the most, you can see what kinds of materials are the most effective. Content at the beginning of the course will also have a higher viewing rate, on average.

- **Least popular content:** This can help you to see what materials might need to be changed or adapted.

- **Time students spend on the platform:** Again, as you seek to improve your course, this figure should go up.

- **Content (audio or video) that is not viewed to completion:** This can help you to see what materials might be too long and need to be subdivided.

- **Forum activity:** These metrics can show you how many students are active, how many discussions are taking place, and how many interactions are student-initiated (a good indicator of engagement).

There are also some helpful individual metrics that you can monitor for each student, in order to see where students may need a little more guidance. These include:

- **The last time the student accessed the course materials:** This metric can allow instructors to send reminders to students who haven't accessed the course within the last 10 days, giving gentle guidance before they fall too far behind.
- **Progress levels:** These metrics can allow instructors to view what percentage of the coursework the student has completed.

Every learning platform offers its own system of analytics. As you seek to understand the specific analytics tools offered by your platform, you can also speak to other instructors who are using the platform to learn how to use them appropriately.

When combined with student feedback, analytical insights can give you a powerful way to see how the course is currently working and how it may be able to be improved.

11. Enhance Your Presentations With Visual Tools

On average, most students in an online course will learn best when strong visual content is provided. Modern students are surrounded by visual content in their everyday lives and some of the most valuable companies in the modern market spend a lot of resources to provide great visual elements, which can add to their consumer appeal. Likewise, having intentional visual tools can add value to your course.

The most common mistake made by online instructors is creating content using black text on a white screen, devoid of any imagery.

According to the Disruptive E-Learning platform, **SH!FT**, there are six reasons why visuals are so powerful in online coursework, as you can see from this image[1].

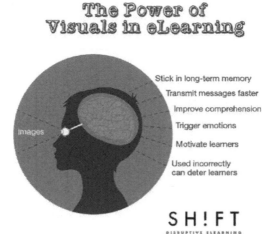

Figure 1.5. Six reasons why visuals are powerful (image credit: shiftelearning.com).

In my personal experience, the most compelling reasons to offer great visual content are because it helps students to retain information long-term, which can positively impact the success of the course, and because visuals can trigger emotions, which personalizes content, enabling students to benefit from a long-lasting learning experience.

12. Understand the Emotional Curve of Your Students During the Course

In education, business, and even our personal lives, emotions influence and impact our levels of commitment to the various tasks we undertake. This is certainly true for online coursework, as well. Many students start the course excited to learn, but experience various ups and downs as their personal schedules change. Students can give in to negative emotions, becoming confused or overwhelmed, and begin to lose interest in the class after the first two to three weeks.

- Recognizing the roles that emotions play for your students can help you to guide them in overcoming these obstacles.

- Encourage your students to become aware of their own emotions toward the topics at hand by offering regular opportunities for reflection and self-assessment. Some topics tend to be more inherently interesting than others, but preconceived ideas about what a topic will entail can negatively influence how dedicated a student may be to that week's assignments.

- Deadline reminders can help students to overcome their initial emotional indifference to a topic, re-engaging them in the coursework.

- Use inspirational stories of the successes of past students to surprise your students. This can help them to see the ways that others have successfully applied the information being covered in their lives and allow them to relate to the aims of the course more directly.

- Be prepared to identify the students who may be struggling or lagging behind, offering support and inspiration.

The key to overcoming the emotional obstacles the students may face in an online course is to remind the students regularly of the future benefits the students will receive from completing the course, which can help them to commit to the tasks at hand in the moment. For any assignment, relate it back to the basic **why** of the course.

13. Motivate Students to Create Something Tangible Related to the Course

One additional activity that has been successful in driving motivation in my own courses is giving students an assignment to create something related to the topic being taught and having them share it with others on the forum. This gives the students a chance to apply the things they have learned in a meaningful way and to make mistakes while in the safety of a learning platform.

For example, when I teach my social media course, students can create short videos in which they test out various mobile apps. This assignment can be repeated in each course, but is highly effective for each set of students that completes it, because it makes the students feel like they have hands-on experience with the tools and topics being discussed.

Whatever kind of course you may be teaching, allow students to create and share their creations with others. Because video is such a personal tool, I recommend tailoring the assignment to use video content when possible.

14. Deliver Engaging and Inspiring Webinars

Webinars and online seminars can be very powerful tools for learning. Due to their effectiveness for students, every online instructor should be familiar with the technology and the best practices for using webinars well in an e-learning environment.

There are a number of benefits that accompany the use of a webinar in the classroom. Students can make a personal connection both to the instructor and to the other students, no matter where they are located, using a computer or a mobile device. Additionally, they can ask questions that are important to them, receive feedback and inspiration, and learn from other students in a social setting.

VIDEO CONFERENCE

Figure 2.6. Webinars.

As you create a plan for your first webinar, it is important to make sure that you have a stable Internet connection and a professional microphone or headset. It is also vital to have a quiet environment for recording, as background noises can be a distraction both to you and your students.

I performed my first webinar back in 2007. Since that time, I have successfully run hundreds of webinars, but also made a lot of mistakes. Here are some of my recommendations for instructors who want to use webinars in their own classrooms:

- **Open up the webinar session at least 10 minutes prior to your planned start time:** By opening up the room a little bit early, you give students a chance to overcome any technological issues that may arise in their connection. Don't be late to your own session, as that sends a message to your students that their time is not as valuable as yours, which is unprofessional.

- **For the first 5 minutes of the session, encourage personal connections:** Use this time to get to know the students present in the webinar, asking them about themselves and allowing any quick questions about the nature of the session to be addressed.

- **Stay on track by sharing the agenda for your webinar:** Give your students the reasons why they should attend the webinar through to the end, what they will get out of the session, and why they should be excited to be there.

- **Use color and creativity on any material presented:** Plan to spend some time working on any visuals or slides that will be presented and avoid having too much text on any one visual. Remember that you can always explain the material verbally during the session.

- **Vary your presentation materials:** If you are using slides, mix in prepared media with live demonstrations, using screensharing tools. For example, in a social media class, you might allow your students to ask a question about a specific website and then provide a live analysis of that website.

- **Engage your students with questions:** To keep engagement with your students, ask a question at least once every 10 minutes. Read out the answers and/or comments that your students send.

- **Involve your audience using short polls:** This helps to keep your material interesting and allows you to share information about the opinions of the students in the session quickly and effectively.

- **Increase participation using short contests:** Keep things fun and light by offering quick challenges for the students who are participating in your webinar.

- **Share inspiring quotes:** This is a great way to keep your students' attention.

- **Be prepared to speak quickly:** When you give a webinar presentation, speak a little more quickly than you would in a physical classroom so that you keep the energy and flow of the content at a decent pace.

- **Allow students to speak:** At some point in your session, unmute your students' microphones and ask their opinions about some of the topics covered. For smaller sessions, you can unmute the microphone channels one by one to ask individual questions, helping students who may be less likely to speak on their own to have an opportunity to share their thoughts.

- **Invite past students to share their own experiences:** Students relate well to past students, so invite successful former students to share tips with the current students.

- **Remind students of any next steps they may need to take:** Offer advice about how the students should use the information in the webinar and communicate any upcoming deadlines.

- **Highlight the ways that students can communicate with you:** Webinars can help to make students more comfortable communicating with their instructor, so take advantage of this by reminding your students of the ways that they can get in touch with you, if needed, after the session ends.

- **Review the analytics:** After every webinar session, analyze your metrics to see how students engaged and discover insights that can be applied to your next webinar.

- **Provide feedback opportunities:** Send a survey to your students so that you can get their input on the ways that your webinar was effective and the ways in which it can be improved.

Because most of the content in an online course is delivered in a flexible manner, it is important to communicate any details about your upcoming webinars well in advance. You can also send them a reminder email as the date approaches, including information on how to participate and how to troubleshoot any basic technical problems that they may encounter.

Using the tips above, you can feel confident that your webinar presentation will help you to connect with your students and engage them in learning in a more active manner.

15. Utilize the Best Tools Available

The world of online learning is constantly changing. The most successful instructors are the ones who stay up-to-date with the available tools, engaging students and helping them to not only complete their coursework, but also meaningfully retain the information received.

While there are a number of great tools on the market today, here are some of the ones that can be the most helpful for online instructors:

Webinar and Online Conferencing Tools

When a course spans a time period of at least five to six weeks, at least one webinar or online conference should be offered. This can give students the chance to ask meaningful questions and learn from each other.

Advance notice of webinar opportunities should be provided to students, but when possible, take the time to record the session and share it for students who may not be able to attend the live session.

The best tools for this are:

- **Facebook Live Video**: This mobile solution is easily accessible for students. The primary drawback for this platform is that the instructor will need to create a page or group for the course in order to use this tool. Groups are generally preferable to pages, simply because of the privacy settings that are available for groups.

- **YouTube Live Stream:** This tool allows instructors to create and embed sessions into the learning portal so that students can directly access the session easily.

- **Adobe Connect:** This is another well-known webinar/conferencing tool that has been used successfully by a number of well-known universities and institutions.

Screensharing Tools

Screensharing offers a unique and quick way to share video content. It provides a wonderful way to respond to specific questions from individual students or to give weekly updates to the whole population of students. Essentially, these tools share a view of your screen with your voice over the top of it.

The best tools for screensharing include:

- Screencastify – *Screencastify.com* : This is a free tool that uses Google Chrome and Google Drive. Instructors can upload their video onto Google Drive and share it with students through email.

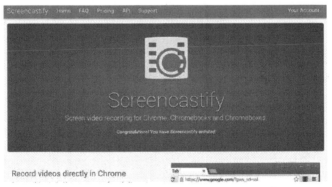

Figure 2.7. Screenrecording tool Screencastify.com.

- Cloud App - *www.getcloudapp.com*: This is a paid tool that allows users to create videos of up to 5 minutes in length of screensharing content, which is then shared via a private link provided to students.

Audio Tools

One of the great things about audio content is that students can listen to it while they are completing other tasks, making it a more portable content type. It is especially helpful for interviews or presentations of certain topics and is especially popular with students who are familiar with podcasts.

Each learning platform tends to have its own plug-ins for audio messages, but another great commercial alternative for short, shared messages is *Audioboo.com*.

File Sharing

Many of the learning platforms include some kind of file sharing tool within their educational package. Other great tools include Dropbox, which is accessible through mobile devices and offers a familiar solution for students, and WeTransfer, which affords the ability to share larger files with your students.

Image Editing Tools

Image editors can allow instructors to create better, more effective visual presentations for their courses.

The best tools for this include:

- *Canva.com*: A free tool with great templates that allow instructors to create professional-looking images without having to use Photoshop. Canva can also be accessed through its iPhone app.

- *Picmonkey.com*: This tool is similar to Canva, but provides several different features. It is great for both students and instructors.

Brainstorming Tools

These tools enable instructors to create mind maps, showcasing information in new and innovative ways.

Current leaders in this type of technology include:

- *Popplet.com*: This site allows instructors to quickly and easily create visually appealing mind maps and diagrams in various colors.

- *Bubbl.us*: This tool is similar to Popplet, but does not have all of the same features.

Other Tools

Messaging apps are another wonderful tool for instructors who want to think outside the box. Many students are already familiar with them, which makes it easy to encourage student involvement.

WhatsApp offers great group and personal communication tools, as does Slack, a relatively new tool used by many startups and businesses. Facebook Messenger can also be used to provide free audio and video calling capabilities, which is helpful not only for teacher-to-student communications, but also student-to-student collaborations.

CHAPTER 2

Artificial Intelligence and Robotics in Education

"Artificial intelligence is the new electricity. Just as 100 years ago electricity transformed industry after industry, artificial intelligence will now do the same."

-Andrew Ng

In its most basic essence, artificial intelligence (AI) refers to computer systems that are able to perform in a way that matches or exceeds human intelligence. Awareness of AI has grown rapidly in the last few years as it has become more developed and more widely adopted. In this chapter, we'll look at a brief overview of AI and how it can be used to improve the field of education.

A Basic Introduction to Artificial Intelligence

Some of the most well-known examples of AI applications include Siri, a personal assistant from Apple, and Watson, an AI application from IMB. These applications are able to understand basic human language and offer communication back to users, whether it be the answer to a question asked or a recommendation for a service. AI will soon be integrated into nearly every part of our lives. AI goes beyond robotics, which is one kind of AI application, but in general many different devices will have AI capabilities in the future.

One interesting element of AI is known as *machine learning*. This is a technology in which computers are able to learn by observing patterns, rather than being programmed directly. Common examples of this include Google's search algorithms, which use machine learning to recognize how and what you search, then offer more relevant and personalized results upon your next search. Facebook's newsfeed is similar, offering customized content based on your previous actions. For example, when you show interest in the posts of a distant relative, Facebook will learn to show you more of that person's content in the future. There are also many applications of machine learning within the field of education, which can make the student experience a more personalized one, but we'll cover that later in this book.

Figure 2.1. Artificial Intelligence.

One unique characteristic of AI development is its potential to grow exponentially. This can be a hard concept for people to grasp, since the average person thinks in a very linear fashion. Perhaps the best way to highlight the idea of the exponential growth of a technology is to use a quote from the well-known AI researcher and futurist Ray Kurzweil:

"Our intuition about the future is linear. But the reality of information technology is exponential, and that makes a profound difference. If I take 30 steps linearly, I get to 30. If I take 30 steps exponentially, I get to a billion."

- Ray Kurzweil

A linear growth pattern may look something like this: 1, 2, 3, 4, 5, 6, 7, 8, 9, 10; while an exponential growth pattern in the same cycle might look like this: 1, 2, 4, 8, 16, 32, 64, 128, 256, 512. You can see the change in value afforded by the exponential growth pattern within the same number of steps.

By following the exponential growth through 30 steps, we would easily get to a billion, as Kurzweil notes. A great number of AI researchers agree that AI will change the world faster than most humans expect and that its impact will be better than we can understand. According to Kurzweil, we should never be afraid of AI, but recognize the opportunities it affords to improve our lives[2]

Negative Connotations About Artificial Intelligence

In recent years, there has been a lot of negativity surrounding the idea of artificial intelligence and robotics through the mainstream media. This is primarily due to the fact that negative news tends to attract more attention and sell more than positive news.

On average, many people do not have enough information about the positive implications and applications that artificial intelligence can bring to our lives.

Here are two of the most recurrent themes that arise from the publicity that promotes skepticism about the use of robotics, and my own opinions about the validity of such claims:

- **Robots will take over the job market:** With the vast advances in technology that have taken place over the past few years, there is a common misconception that robots could completely take over the job market, taking jobs away from people who once were needed to complete certain tasks. However, anyone studying the business market today should recognize that technology has always been a job creator. With new advances in technology come new opportunities in the job market. However, it is likely that in the future, robots using AI technology will perform many of the jobs that currently relate to manual labor. With the rise of autonomous, self-driving cars, for example, fewer truck drivers and taxi drivers will be needed, especially within the city centers of the world. As this occurs, governments and institutions should be involved in the re-education of workers who may need to learn new skills to continue to actively participate in the job market.

Probably the most accurate interpretation of the effects that artificial intelligence will have comes from Kevin Kelly, who confirms that the rise of AI and robotics are related to productivity. According to Kelly, as AI becomes more capable and efficient, it is likely that all productivity tasks will be done by robotics. However, many new and exciting jobs are also likely to come along with this change.[3]

- **Robots will eventually become dangerous to humans:** This idea has been a popular one in science fiction for a number of years because it makes for a dramatic storyline. However, in reality, the nature of robotics makes it very unlikely that these science fiction ideas will ever play out in real life. Some of the largest companies that are currently developing artificial intelligence tools and applications are Facebook, Alphabet (formerly known as Google), IBM, Microsoft, and Amazon. Currently, their researchers are working together in order to discuss the impact that AI can have across a multitude of sectors, including transportation, business, and welfare[4].

It is important to take artificial intelligence and robotics seriously, but even more vital that instructors seek to spread information about the new opportunities that are likely to be generated from these amazing technologies.

As a whole, the people who will be the most successful in the markets affected by the growth of artificial intelligence and robotics are the ones who welcome it and recognize the amazing implications it has for life as we know it.

This chapter has focused on some of the applications that artificial intelligence has within the realm of education, but there are many ways in which artificial intelligence will continue to be applied in every industry, impacting many of the things that we do every day.

The greatest potential drawbacks to the new artificial intelligence capabilities include social issues like the tracking and protecting of our private information, something that those involved in the creation of new technology will need to consider.

While this is not a comprehensive picture of the implications and applications of artificial intelligence, but rather a snapshot of the possibilities that these technologies will offer to the field of education, instructors should be eager to explore the potential opportunities afforded by these new tools.

How Artificial Intelligence Will Help Students

As you consider the ways that you can use technology for education, the learning objectives set out for the students should be your priority and the technology should be the means to achieve it, rather than making the technology itself a priority.

When it comes to artificial intelligence within education, the emphasis is not so much on the traditional idea of physical robot as it is on the idea of cloud-based technologies created with and through machines built to assist people in their daily tasks.

Historically, one of the biggest obstacles faced by educators is the model of the traditional classroom, in which a single lecture is given to a multitude of students without any knowledge of their previous experience with the topic at hand. Within a single classroom, there may be several very motivated students and others who have very low motivation.

Artificial intelligence can help instructors to change all of that, offering personalized learning experiences to students that are more effective than ever before. With new tools, instructors can customize the learning experience to their students' individual needs and capabilities. Many universities are just beginning to explore the impact these technologies can provide and finding a great deal of success through applying artificial intelligence.

Here are four of the top ways that artificial intelligence can be used to teach and train students:

- **Personalized learning platforms:** Imagine a course where 30 students begin to learn about the same topic online, but rather than having the same experience, the course could be personalized in 30 different ways, customized to the previous knowledge and skill of each student, making it a more enjoyable and successful learning experience. Not only could individual students study at their own pace, but instructors could also provide personalized feedback, support and motivation, reducing the rates of students who drop out. As a result, each of the 30 students could experience some level of meaningful success through the course.

From my own experience, sharing success stories from past students is a key factor in these kinds of platforms, as these positive role models can inspire and motivate students in the e-learning environment.

Through these kinds of personalized platforms that leverage artificial intelligence, students and instructors can enjoy a high degree of efficiency and success.

- **Individualized artificial intelligence tutors:** One application of this kind of tutor would be a personalized AI teaching assistant created to answer basic questions students ask of it regarding a given topic (such as deadlines or formats for assignments), provide motivation to keep up with coursework as needed, and provide information about the university or institution.

In most cases, these tools could be run through voice recognition software, which would allow the students to speak directly to the AI tutor. They could also employ results from personality tests and other informational data to personalize results to the student.

As life expectancies increase and people continue to seek out learning opportunities, future students may also benefit from life-long AI tutors as the technology develops. The most advanced versions of these AI tutors may be able to understand emotional undertones in communications and make recommendations based not just upon what is said, but also upon how things are said.

This kind of AI teaching assistant has already been used for testing at Georgia Tech, where AI software powered by IBM's Watson was able to answer student questions on forums with a high degree of success. In most cases, students didn't even notice that the response given did not come from a human source[5].

Again, as these tools are employed, privacy concerns with the tracking of personal information will need to be considered.

- **Personalized games:** Several recent studies have revealed that playing games can be one of the best ways to learn something new. Generating effective games can require a lot of time and creativity, which can be challenging.

As we employ artificial intelligence tools, the creation of these kinds of games will become easier, allowing instructors to customize games to their students' personalities and pedagogical needs. With these highly entertaining games, students will benefit from increased motivation and enjoyment of the topics being taught.

- **Crafting a more enjoyable learning experience:** Another potential benefit of AI in the field of education is its ability to keep students engaged in the coursework by making the experience a more fun one. It is easy to see that students who have fun while they learn tend to remember the material better, making the content more effective. In the future, learning platforms powered by AI will be able to create interactive tools designed to continuously engage the learner, dispelling boredom and lack of motivation.

How Artificial Intelligence Will Assist Teachers in Their Work

Within the next few years, the nature of teaching will likely change as AI technology improves. While some experts claim that artificial intelligence will render teachers obsolete, I disagree. I do believe, however, that the role instructors will play in the classroom is likely to change as both teachers and students start to use AI technology to study and instruct in more effective ways. As a whole, I believe that this technology, when properly applied, can have substantial positive effects within the realm of education.

There may be some very basic courses in which AI-based programs can perform the role of the instructor. This may lead to a need for fewer teachers, but teachers will always be needed in some capacity. More likely than not, what is required from teachers will change and responsibilities will start to shift, as teachers become more like career mentors or life coaches to their students.

As this shift occurs, emotional and social intelligence will be primary qualifications of the instructors, along with academic knowledge and skill. Teachers will be able to check in on their students, providing inspiration and motivation, while delegating some aspects of the instruction to AI programs. Students will always need some degree of human interaction in order to learn, but the kinds of interaction offered by teachers will probably change with the advances in technology.

New technologies are already being employed at a number of learning institutions and universities. Here are few of the ways that AI is likely to change the nature of teachers' work in the future:

- **Grading:** Within the traditional classroom, grading can be complex, taking up a great deal of time. Additionally, the volume and type of work necessary for grading increases the possibility of human error in the grading process.

  As AI technology continues to develop, students and teachers will benefit from the availability of more data points and complex trend monitoring, offering final grades that can be based on multiple factors. When this technology is first implemented, it will need to be closely monitored to ensure that the results are accurate, but over time, AI technology may even be able to take in student responses to questions through speech recognition.

Even now, AI technology is being used for the grading of typed assignments and multiple choice tests. As new advances are offered, instructors will be better able to focus on individual students and provide an even higher degree of quality education to each student.

One of the companies that is seeking to solve the problems of traditional grading in an innovative way is GradeScope (www.gradescope.com). Many top universities in the USA, including UC Berkeley, Stanford and MIT, currently use this program to aid their teachers.

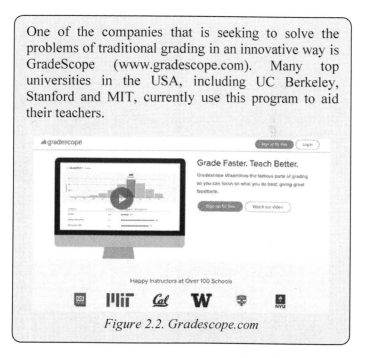

Figure 2.2. Gradescope.com

At the moment, this company is developing an artificial intelligence component that will help teachers to offer grades in a faster, more effective way. In most cases, students like these kinds of grading systems because they provide more detailed, in-depth feedback, helping them to improve in their coursework and study habits.

- **Teachers will benefit from AI-based assistants:** Currently, teachers who instruct in online courses have to spend a lot of time analyzing the metrics that are available through the various online platforms, which are limited.

  AI-based assistants can provide a tremendous amount of detail to instructors, allowing them to pinpoint students who may need additional help, while challenging advanced students more appropriately. These tools will also make it easy for instructors to identify the ways that they can improve the effectiveness of their courses over time.

- AI assistants may also help teachers to develop creative tools, like games, to design exciting learning opportunities for their students. Personally, I would love to offer my students games that were built around the topics I teach, but this would be incredibly time consuming and would be a challenge to create in terms of the technology. As the AI technology is developed further, students will be able to benefit from personalized games that can be created with less effort on the part of the instructor.

As each aspect of the AI technology improves, instructors can experiment with the opportunities afforded by artificial intelligence, implementing new tools gradually and observing the results for the students in their care.

Knewton – an Example of Adaptive Learning

In adaptive learning you use computers as interactive teaching devices. One of the most innovative companies in the adaptive learning space is Knewton, which offers a free and open adaptive learning experience.

According to their website, *"Knewton is a textbook that pinpoints material to improve your education and save you time by adapting to your personal learning style and knowledge to deliver an experience unique to your needs. With every question you answer, Knewton will adapt to deliver a more and more effective experience."*

This is how Jose Ferreira, the founder and CEO of Knewton, describes it: *"Knewton plucks the perfect bits of content for you from the cloud and assembles them according to the ideal learning strategy for you, as determined by the combined data-power of millions of other students. Think of it as a friendly robot-tutor in the sky*[6]*"*

You can find more information on their website *www.knewton.com* and sign up to test it out. In the future there will be several similar adaptive learning tools, but for now Knewton is probably the most well-known and advanced

New Opportunities in Global Education & Potential Drawbacks to Social Development

As AI-enhanced learning platforms continue to evolve, there will be a greater number of opportunities in parts of the world that are less developed, opening up access to high-quality education in a more affordable and effective way than is currently available.

When this happens, I believe that large companies like Google, Facebook, Amazon, Microsoft, and IBM will start to offer platforms that offer basic education at a reduced or minimal cost, opening up doors for hundreds of thousands of students to learn simultaneously.

Because we are still in the early days of artificial intelligence applications, there are still a number of problems to be solved and questions to be answered regarding this technology. One potential consequence of learning through AI tools is the lack of socialization that often accompanies a high degree of screen time. In turn, this may create a feeling of isolation in students, which can lead to other problems.

According to a report by Stanford University published in September of 2016 called **Artificial Intelligence and Life in 2030:**

"On the negative side, there is already a major trend among students to restrict their social contacts to electronic ones and to spend large amounts of time

without social contact, interacting with online programs. If education also occurs more and more online, what effect will the lack of regular, face-to-face contact with peers have on students' social development?"[7]

Expert interview with Topi Litmanen from Claned

Figure 2.3. Claned.com

Claned is a learning management platform which combines artificial intelligence and social learning and is currently used by the United Nations, Microsoft, and many other organizations. Topi Litmanen from Claned shared this comment with us:

*"Our mission is to bring the most **effective educational theories** and **social media tools** to learning, combined with the best **Finnish pedagogical practices** and artificial intelligence.*

Artificial intelligence opens up whole new possibilities for the future of learning. Claned has the ability to learn how different students learn and personalizes learning to match their individual needs and preferences. This improves learning motivation and results. In addition, teachers who use Claned gain comprehensive insights into students' study performances and learning orientations, as well as their motivations, emotions and stress levels.

We also value social learning, which excites and motivates students nowadays. For example, when Oulu Business School used Claned, the amount of social collaboration increased by over 500%, compared to everything else they had tried before. The students sent over 5,000 chat messages on Claned during the first week of the course."

-Topi Litmanen, PhD, Chief Educational Scientist,
Claned.com

CHAPTER 3

Virtual Reality and Augmented Reality in Education

"We are making a long-term bet that immersive, virtual and augmented reality will become a part of people's daily life"

- Mark Zuckerberg

According to Google, virtual reality is a *"computer-generated simulation of a three-dimensional image or environment that can be interacted with in a seemingly real or physical way by a person using special electronic equipment, such as a helmet with a screen inside or gloves fitted with sensors."*

Introduction to Virtual Reality

Have you ever tried a virtual reality headset? The first time I tried it, I was surprised. I had originally thought that virtual reality was mainly targeted toward gamers or young children, so when I put on the headset, I was amazed by the results.

All of a sudden, I was having a meal with an indigenous family in the mountains of Peru. With the click of another button, I was visiting the International Space Station. The virtual reality experience was both immersive and impactful.

There are a number of different virtual reality headsets. The high-end models are the Oculus Rift (which is owned by Facebook), the PlayStation VR, and the HTC Vive. Currently, these headsets are fairly expensive, averaging just under $600 USD, but as the technology develops, these prices are likely to go down, opening up the virtual reality experience for a greater number of users.

Figure 3.1. Oculus Rift
(image credit www.oculus.com/press-kit/hardware).

On the less expensive end of the spectrum, Google Cardboard is a simple virtual reality viewer that can be used with other headsets. My personal favorite is the VR ShineCon, which runs under $20 online and works with your smartphone.

At the moment, virtual reality headsets are owned by only a small percentage of the population, but as prices continue to drop, their use is likely to become more common. In fact, as smartphones are able to have better processing power, virtual reality may come to mobile devices, as well.

In general, virtual reality offers amazing benefits for the field of education, which we'll explore in a bit.

Advantages and Disadvantages of Virtual Reality

Here are some of the primary advantages offered by virtual reality:

- Power to share **real-life experiences** in an immersive manner.

- **Additional opportunities for sales and marketing** in different business sectors including real estate, tourism, interior design, and more.

- Ability to **experience the benefits of travel** with lower cost.

- **Greater opportunities for career training** and advancement within companies.

- **Medical benefits**, including rehabilitation experiences for conditions like depression.

There are also some potential drawbacks to the use of virtual reality technologies, which can include:

- **Potential for motion sickness with extended use:** When an individual uses a virtual reality headset for an extended period of time, they may experience something known as vestibular-ocular conflict, also called "simulator sickness." A number of researchers are currently working to find a solution to this problem, but it is one of the key concerns of people who might otherwise be interested in using this tool.

- **Resistance to new technologies:** In many instances, instructors can be opposed to bringing in new technologies, fearful that they may be expensive, hard to learn, or that they may change the dynamics of the classroom as they know them.

- **Lack of long-term studies on the impacts of virtual reality** on the people who use it often. Some experts advise that children under the age of 18 should not use this technology, as it may impact brain development.

- **Potential to lose track of actual reality when virtual reality is used too often.**

- **Possible development of insomnia, anxiety, or other health concerns.**

- **Lack of social and emotional skills** for people who use virtual reality to escape their daily lives.

- **Possible negative applications**, including gang communications or illicit activities.

As with any technology, there are benefits and drawbacks to the use of virtual reality. Because of this, there are some basic guidelines that will need to be developed and shared amongst the community of people using virtual reality in the near future.

Virtual Reality in the Field of Education

In general, the use of virtual reality technologies in the field of education is fairly new. Because of the expense associated with it, not all educational institutions have access to this kind of experience for their students. However, as the technology continues to evolve and prices decrease, teaching with virtual reality is likely to become more commonplace.

The potential for this technology is really unlimited, so the teachers who are able to use virtual reality most effectively will be the ones who embrace it early and are willing to be creative in its use.

Figure 3.2. Virtual Reality in education.

Some of the potential benefits to the use of virtual reality in education include:

- **Powerful emotional experiences for students:** One of the key reasons why virtual reality has so much potential impact in education is that it can be used to affect emotions. When we have an emotional experience, we tend to store that experience in our memory. For students, this means that they will learn more effectively and quickly. They will also enjoy a much more immersive experience when exposed to content through virtual reality instead of traditional textbooks or even video lectures.

- **Increased motivation:** Because of the exciting, effective nature of virtual reality technologies, students involved in courses that use it well will likely have a greater degree of motivation, become more engaged in the assignments, and have a decreased chance of dropping out of the course prior to completion. Also the general drop-out rates in universities may decrease if virtual reality is used as a teaching tool for students who need special training[8].

- **Less time in training:** With greater impact than more traditional methods, students using virtual reality will likely be able to learn complex information in less time, which means that the time required to be spent in training for a career will decrease.

- **Stronger educational experiences through simulations:** Nearly any action that a person can do can be simulated through virtual reality. Imagine a course in which medical students could try their hand at a surgery without any risk or where future chemists could play with the properties of an element safely while in the classroom. There are endless possibilities to the ways in which this technology can be used.

- **Greater efficiency with time and resources:** Because students will be able to practice their skills virtually, whether they are preparing to fly an airplane or drive a car, there are huge potential environmental savings to be gained from this technology.

- **Opportunities to experience new cultures:** It can be difficult for a person to truly understand and empathize with someone from another culture. By being able to share in experiences from other cultures, virtual reality technologies will help to students to see the value in experiences shared by others.

- **Ability to create specialized learning plans:** Virtual reality can be a helpful tool to encourage and mentally stimulate students who need additional motivation in the classroom. By engaging the senses more fully, the impact of the material taught can be greater, while customizing the lesson to the needs of the student.

- **More access to education:** With prices for virtual headsets decreasing, this technology will open up education in powerful ways to new populations of students.

These are just a few of the core benefits that are associated with virtual reality, but new benefits and opportunities will likely be discovered as the technology improves. To grasp the full potential of virtual reality in education, every university or institution should try to develop its own virtual learning environments, asking for student feedback and insight along the way to inspire creativity and leverage student motivation.

How to Begin Using 360-Degree Photos to Create Virtual Reality Content

With new innovations in video and photo technology, instructors should start becoming familiar with 360-degree photos and videos. Currently, Facebook supports these kinds of videos, which have become more important tools for businesses. 360-degree photos and videos are becoming more widely known in the mainstream markets, as well.

Using 360-degree photos within a learning environment can aid more visual learners and give students great tools to understand complex concepts. There are a number of iPhone and Android apps that can help instructors to capture 360-degree photos.

ThingLink is one portal through which educators can create and share engaging and interactive images, videos, and 360-degree photos with custom annotations. It helps educators to take advantage of a digital storytelling culture, allowing students to design their own 360-degree images, which can then be viewed using a virtual reality device, like Google Cardboard. Ulla Engeström is the founder and CEO of ThingLink and shares with us her vision about how to use this tool.

Expert interview – ULLA ENGESTRÖM

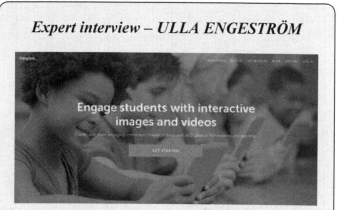

Figure 3.3. ThingLink (image credit
www.thinglink.com/edu)

1. What benefits do 360 photos and videos bring to education?

There are several powerful possibilities that exist for teaching and learning with 360-degree photos and videos. First, 360 degree media - especially when viewed with virtual reality headsets - encourage exploration by providing students with a participatory experience of a place, whether that may be a foreign city, a space station, a human body, a new school, or a museum that is otherwise closed to the public.

This ability to virtually visit any place on Earth any time will radically change the way we acquire and construct new knowledge. Initial interest among teachers shows that 360 photos efficiently support teaching vocabulary in the different subject areas, and this improves students' comprehension and overall success in school.

Also, when teachers and students can personalize 360 experiences with their own notes, observations, close-up photos, and audio and video recordings, 360 photos transform into a new kind of storytelling and learning platform. More than the ready-made virtual reality tours or expeditions, it is the creation of a virtual reality story that holds a great potential for learning. It develops a student's critical thinking and ability to search for and combine various types of knowledge, and improves practical skills in multimedia production and presentation.

2. Why are 360 photos and videos becoming so important in higher education?

As the web becomes more visual, images and videos will have a bigger role in everything we do, including education. Virtual reality in education has been a topic since the 1990s, but the recent development in omnidirectional camera technology, CPUs, and affordable headsets have made the technology accessible for schools in a new way.

When 360 cameras become more common so that they are integrated in our phones and tablet devices, anyone can become a content creator for virtual reality. Teachers and students are paving the way for a new generation of user generated 360 content that spreads from education to social, commerce, and entertainment.

360 streaming will have a tremendous impact on the accessibility of higher education worldwide.

3. What benefits have educators gained from using ThingLink?

The creation of interactive images and videos with ThingLink has provided students with a variety of ways to demonstrate learning and practice good digital citizenship through the use and combination of various types of digital materials.

Teachers have used ThingLink to build in data collection for assessment and planning. For example, they have enriched existing educational videos and images with content to actively engage students, and provide them with additional resources for personalized learning. Teachers have also been creative in integrating 3rd party tools such as entry and exit questionnaires made with Google Forms in images and videos.

The creation of interactive images has extended learning beyond the classroom walls. Students have taken phones or tablets to field trips and collected materials for interactive documentaries, nature paths, and 360 degree audio tours.

Theoretical discussion on the benefits of interactive media creation in the classroom linked to studies of the multiple forms of intelligence, as well as studies on how the use of images in learning supports memory and cognitive development.

- Ulla Engeström, CEO, ThingLink.com

nstructors who wish to create 360-degree videos can take advantage of several options in video cameras, including Ricoh Theta S or 360fly 4K. These cameras can be used to shoot 360-degree video content, which can later be uploaded to Facebook or YouTube and used for educational purposes. While most of the current consumer 360-degree cameras do not offer high-quality images, stronger tools are currently in development that will be available to educators in the future. However, teachers who want to learn to use this technology now can already begin to create their own virtual reality content with one of these existing cameras.

Introduction to Augmented Reality

By one of the most common definitions, augmented reality (AR) occurs when elements of virtual reality are combined with real-life elements. In virtual reality, a person can experience a completely different world, but in augmented reality, that same person would encounter real-life objects with an overlay of computer-generated images.

Figure 3.4. Augmented Reality.

Perhaps the most well-known example of augmented reality is the mobile game Pokémon Go, which was released in July 2016 and quickly reached over 100 million downloads. This game uses your smartphone camera and GPS to play a game in which you catch "pocket monsters" in certain geographical locations. Pokémon Go represents a prime example of the ways that augmented reality can be used, bringing fantastical creatures to life in the real world. This game has become very popular, as it offers great visual components and encourages its players to get outside and venture into new places.

Augmented Reality in Education

There are currently many applications that are available for augmented reality. It can be a powerful tool in a learning environment, offering unique opportunities for self-guided education on field trips by displaying real-world environments with information provided as an overlay. It can also be used to build engaging games for students to play as they learn.

Augmented reality affords a different kind of learning environment that cannot be matched. While virtual reality gives impressive experiences of other worlds, augmented reality brings unique elements into the world directly around you.

One disadvantage to augmented reality as it currently stands is that it relies on the use of a device, like a smartphone, that is not fully optimized to be used in this way. For example, playing Pokémon Go for an extended period of time can drain battery life and requires stable connectivity to the Internet. However, this will likely be overcome as mobile technology advances, offering stronger processing power, longer battery life, and better connectivity features.

The future of augmented reality probably lies in hardware and software that is based on the idea of glasses. In a recent conference, Mark Zuckerberg, founder of Facebook, spoke to an audience in Lagos, Nigeria, casting a vision of a future in which people would live with these kinds of augmented reality glasses, performing everyday tasks like watching TV, using apps on the device that provide imagery projected onto a wall nearby[9].

As Zuckerberg pointed out, this kind of technology will likely open up new doors in education, where students could experience a visual of the instructor right there in their home environment while experiencing high-quality educational content.

There are many opportunities that will be available through this new technology, so instructors should be prepared to think through the applications and potentials of this new way of teaching.

Introduction to Mixed Reality

In many ways, mixed reality is very similar to augmented reality. Tech journalist Eric Johnson describes the idea of mixed reality like this:

Mixed reality lets the user see the real world (like AR) while also seeing believable, virtual objects (like VR). And then it anchors those virtual objects to a point in real space, making it possible to treat them as "real," at least from the perspective of the person who can see the MR experience[10].

One of the most well-known mixed reality applications is called Hololens and is available from Microsoft. This tool allows you to see the real world with the addition of high definition holograms or 3D images. Microsoft named this technology *holographic computing*. Their main goal for this tool is to develop it into a platform that can replace traditional computers so that everyone will be able to access Windows while wearing the Hololens device.

There are a number of potential applications for this kind of technology in education. Like with virtual reality, nearly anything can be simulated with this technology, making it possible to design unique and innovative learning environments in which students and teachers can participate actively in the creation of new worlds.

Most likely, Hololens and similar devices will be used in medical studies, tourism, and architectural engineering, but will probably also expand into other fields of study. It will be an amazing tool for specialized learning environments.

One of the most fascinating forecasts of the potentials for future holographic computing comes from James Mackie, who predicts that in a span of seven years, we will no longer have the need for mobile devices, monitors, keyboards, or mice, instead viewing everything through specialized devices that project images onto walls[11].

Another company that is also attempting to change the field of mixed reality is Magic Leap. With a new mixed reality headset ready to launch soon, this business has already raised over $1.39 billion. Without a physical product on the market or a lot of information about the specifics of their technology, this company is already valued at roughly $3.5 billion.

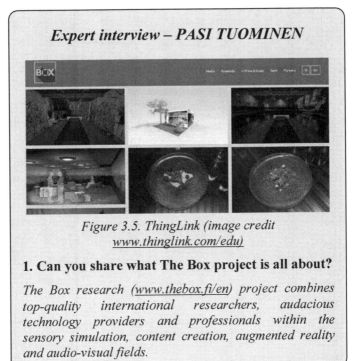

Figure 3.5. ThingLink (image credit www.thinglink.com/edu)

1. Can you share what The Box project is all about?

The Box research (www.thebox.fi/en) project combines top-quality international researchers, audacious technology providers and professionals within the sensory simulation, content creation, augmented reality and audio-visual fields.

1. Can you share what The Box project is all about?

The Box research (www.thebox.fi/en) project combines top-quality international researchers, audacious technology providers and professionals within the sensory simulation, content creation, augmented reality and audio-visual fields.

In The Box students can try to test different service simulations and situations in real life using augmented reality or mixed reality. The experiences so far have been very positive. We believe in learning by development as all phases are documented and knowledge evolves in an ongoing process and in real time. Students have done different learning cases and experiments; for example, there has been a virtual sauna experience and a virtual wedding. The next project is called "Coffee Moment Experience," where we test how an augmented reality experiment works with Starbucks surroundings mixed with real life Starbucks coffee & baristas.

2. What makes learning using augmented reality better than typical classroom learning?

One key element of The Box project is involving students and providing them with the tools (the technology) and a white canvas to create their own projects, so that they can show their own skills, unique talents and enthusiasm. Furthermore, learning in this type of environment helps them learn the tolerance of mistakes, which is essential in today's business life. Additionally, the ideology of fast prototyping and learning by doing is of great importance and helps students to become more relevant in tomorrow's job market.

3. How do you see the future of service and hospitality business education with the growth of all the new emerging technologies?

We need to recognize the vast array of technological innovations and their acceptance by the millennial generation and Generation Z. Education must follow this stream and adapt to their needs and wants.

Due to the virtually limitless computing power availability at very low cost through cloud computing, digitalization will expand exponentially. Therefore, it is expected that service and hospitality business education will embrace at least mobile technology, Internet of Things (IoT), robotics/drones, Artificial Intelligence (AI), 3D-printing, and Virtual/Augmented Reality (VR/AR). Hospitality businesses will rely heavily on computer technology, and on-demand services and experiences will increase as businesses attempt to profit from the 24/7 Now Economy. This is why we are already teaching in augmented and mixed reality learning environments so that the students get first-hand experience with these technologies.

- Pasi Tuominen - Customer Experience Professional, Educator and Lecturer at HAAGA-HELIA University of Applied Sciences

CHAPTER 4

Future of Skills in Education

"The future belongs to those who learn more skills and combine them in creative ways."

- Robert Greene

In the modern workforce, the particular skills that are necessary to success are changing rapidly. With great strides being made in technology and the continued digitalization of nearly every aspect of our lives, we will soon see changes in how people communicate, do business, participate in leisure activities, and even sleep.

These advances can lead people to become overwhelmed and confused about what they need in order to be successful on the job market. This can lead them to resist technological changes. As a whole, however, these developments will offer a greater number of opportunities, especially as people begin to recognize their importance.

In this section, I'll share my views on the skills that I believe are vital to success in the modern educational field. Designing curriculum with an eye towards the future can be a challenging and complex process, as there are many elements and changing variables to consider. This is especially true when students are asked to study a topic that may seem relevant and important when they begin their education, but may be obsolete or unnecessary by the time that they graduate.

In order to truly be relevant to the job market of the near future, I've compiled a list of skills and talents that will be helpful to students, regardless of the specific topic that they are studying. Many universities are including these same skills in their curriculum and these same skills will follow students into the workforce.

As you'll see in the list below, the skills are divided into the categories of "people skills" and "business skills." While these two areas may sometimes converge, this separation is designed to offer a clearer overview of the skills included.

People Skills For the Future

1. **Self-awareness and self-assessment:** I first encountered the benefits to self-assessment when I began my studies at Haaga-Helia Business Polytechnics in Helsinki, Finland, in 2001. Before that time, I had experience in studying international business in Mexico and Italy that offered advanced business techniques, but had not yet come across this tool.

   In today's rapidly changing and complex world, self-awareness is extremely valuable, helping people to recognize their full potential and areas that might need to be improved. It can also help people to identify and accept their uniqueness, which can add self-esteem and motivation for learning. This skill is particularly valuable for entrepreneurs and freelancers.

In one of my online courses, I ask the students to do what is known as a "personal SWOT analysis," which includes analysis of strengths, weaknesses, and opportunities within a particular area of their lives. To my surprise, it has become one of the most popular activities that we do, as the students feel that it is truly beneficial. It can be helpful to teach this skill to students using personality tests, which can help them to get started in self-assessment.

Figure 4.1. Self-awareness.

2. **Emotional Intelligence:** By one common definition, emotional intelligence is one's capacity to be aware of and express emotions. It is quite useful in interpersonal relationships.

As the business world becomes more complex, the people with high emotional intelligence will be able to get ahead faster. Historically, showing or talking about emotions was once viewed as a sign of weakness in many cultures, but in recent years, more and more professionals are starting to discover the benefits of emotional intelligence. I personally believe that we are only beginning to discover the power of this skill.

3. **Social Intelligence:** This skill relates to how one is able to interact with others in various situations. It involves a basic understanding of the thoughts and opinions in others. In a world where work within small, globally distributed teams is growing, social intelligence can help students to become familiar with the needs of working with different kinds of people, while maintaining their workflow through obstacles as they arise. Another aspect of this particular skill is to develop or join a peer group that can provide support and excitement for the projects that you undertake.

4. **Interpersonal Intelligence:** The ways that we communicate and socialize with our close family and friends can actually help us to have a more balanced life and a greater sense of well-being and happiness. This in turn allows you to offer greater efforts towards your work. For this to happen, we should limit time spent on devices and increase the time that we spend with those who are important to us on a personal level.

5. **Empathy and Active Listening:** Maintaining a deep understanding of the ways that people experience things will help us to move forward

in business and in our personal lives. The ability to be patient and value another person's perspective allows us to gain insight into various situations. This combination of empathy and active listening will be vital in the future workforce.

6. **Cultural Flexibility:** This is the ability to adapt to new cultures and new ways of working and living quickly. This goes beyond cultural understanding, allowing people to be flexible when they encounter different belief systems and cultural values. In the past, people who were the most well-travelled had the most potential to have cultural flexibility, but as technology advances, this skill will be more readily available through virtual reality training programs.

7. **Perseverance and Passion:** Angela Duckworth, an American psychologist and author of the best-selling book <u>Grit: The Power of Passion and Perseverance</u>, argues that the most important predictor of success is something she calls "grit," which is the passion and perseverance for long-term goals. Many students pursue quick fixes and instant gratification, so teaching patience for long-term gratification is vital. One way to teach this skill is to share inspiring role models and case studies of people who have had success, especially when the examples offered relate in some way to what the students are learning.

Figure 4.2. Passion.

8. **A Focus on the Common Good:** Recognizing the value of the common good, rather than simply focusing on individual wants and needs, can help students to work together. American author and philanthropist Anthony Robbins says it this way: "Life is not about me; it's about we." In most cases, working towards the common good has been shown to give people a higher degree of satisfaction than primarily seeking their own benefit.

9. **Mindfulness and Meditation:** I truly believe this should be a mandatory subject in every university and institution. There are countless studies that show the benefits of these practices, and there are more and more stories of high achievers in various industries (sports, business, finance, and more) finding success through mindfulness and meditation. It is easy to start learning these skills, simply by looking for relevant videos on YouTube.

10. **Physical Training:** Maintaining physical balance can help you to enjoy clarity, mental focus, and a healthier life in general. As people begin to spend more time in front of the screen, physical motion will become even more vital.

11. **Storytelling:** Storytelling is one of the most natural ways for humans to communicate with each other with common understanding. Thousands of years ago, storytelling was the primary form of communication and this same form is still very helpful today. Stories are powerful tools to evoke emotion and to understand complex situations. According to one study, 92% of consumers want brands to create ads that have a storytelling component[12] There are many opportunities to use storytelling in creative communication and it is likely that those who excel in this art will be in high demand in the future job markets.

Business Skills For the Future

12. **Problem Solving:** *The Future of Jobs* report from World Economy Forums highlights the importance of complex problem solving skills in the world of business. This skill is more relevant than ever due to the speed of technological innovation and the changing nature of the way that people do business. Problem solving skills can help people to understand their co-workers, environments, and even tools and machines that they interact with[13].

13. **Creativity:** It is easy to overlook this simple skill, but it will be a critical part of many career markets going forward. The leading expert in applying creativity to education is Sir Ken Robinsson, who is quoted as saying, *"Creativity is putting your imagination to work, and it's produced the most extraordinary results in human culture."*

    As more technology is introduced into business and education, it will become even more important for people to develop unique and innovative ways to implement that technology. To learn more about the value of creativity, consider reading some of the books available from Robinsson, which include The Element: How Finding Your Passion Changes Everything and Creative Schools: The Grassroots Revolution that's Transforming Education.

14. **Adaptability to New Technology:** Moving forward, the people who are willing and able to adapt to new technologies and the opportunities that they provide are going to have the best orientation towards success, while those who resist new technologies are likely to fall behind or miss out. While it is important for universities to show students how to be proactive in new technologies, they should also put resources to training teachers about creative ways to use technology within the classroom.

15. **Entrepreneurial Mindset:** Within the next 5 years, advancements in robotics and machinery will likely change the kinds of jobs available on

the job market. People who have strong entrepreneurial skills and know how to seek advice in the right places will be able to experience the benefits of these changes. Having the idea that anything is possible can help a person to leverage their talents and skills to jumpstart a business quickly and effectively.

16. **Sales and Marketing:** More than ever before, people are creating businesses centered in their passions. For this to work, they need to understand the fundamentals of sales and marketing techniques, including how to communicate what they can offer and how to acquire new customers. This is particularly important for students who take a more traditional educational path, but may later want to start their own business.

17. **Data Analysis:** According to Clive Humby, "Data is the oil of the 21st century." As more things become digitalized, data analysis becomes an increasingly important skill. Even in the current market, entrepreneurs who wish to market their business need to understand how to correctly interpret analytics offered through Google Analytics, Facebook Insights, YouTube Insights, and more, as well as how to come to appropriate conclusions about the data to drive future business decisions. While you may think that this skill is only for "geeks," the enhanced capabilities of artificial intelligence and rise of new technologies means that the ability to

analyze data effectively will be a primary tool for those in the job market in the near future.

18. **Presentation Skills:** One important business skill that is not likely to change in the future is the ability to speak and present to diverse groups of people. The people who master this skill often find themselves in leadership positions, both on smaller projects and on larger teams. It is important for educators to foster the growth of students when it comes to presentation skills, both in person and in digital formats. The ability to motivate and inspire others will be important for many years to come.

Figure 4.3. Presentation skills.

19. **Environmental Intelligence:** As people begin to consider the value of preserving resources over time, it will be important for them to understand how technology can make that happen. The growing use of solar energy solutions and even self-driven cars can help to make a large difference environmentally. Finding value in our common resources should be a skill that is taught to students early and often.

20. **Large-Scale Thinking:** As the world becomes ever more connected, the ability to think about and analyze large entities becomes vital. While it is important to be able to consider the small details of a project, big picture thinking that accounts for complexities and interwoven elements will be valuable and should be highly emphasized in the world of education.

21. **Accounting and Money Management:** Not only can basic accounting principles help people within their personal lives, but it can also help them to understand the complexities of starting, running, or participating in a business. While money management is not one of the traditional courses found in universities, more and more educational institutions are recognizing the value of these kinds of skills. Regardless of your educational background or career ambitions, this skill is necessary to success. Additionally, those who have a more comprehensive understanding of finances often have more balance within their lives as a whole.

22. **The Ability to Unplug:** As strange as it may seem to include this as a business skill, consider the fact that it is becoming harder to find places that don't have Internet connections nowadays. People who are able to disconnect from their devices and connect in more intimate ways with others will experience greater joy and less stress than those who are addicted to their devices. In the current generation, many people lack this

skill and could benefit from instruction in how to become better at it.

23. **Spotting Trends:** In a rapidly changing world, being able to recognize signals of potential opportunities in the future is immensely helpful. Not only is this skill accessible to people of all backgrounds, but it can also help entrepreneurs to take advantage of business ventures, simply by learning how to see trends and implement practices at the right time. For example, with the rise of self-driving cars, someone may start to think through the ways that this technology can be utilized in a creative way.

24. **Design thinking and design mindset:** In the future we will have products and services that we cannot even image today. Design mindset is solution-focused approach where you find desired solutions to complex problems. This is a skill that everyone can learn and will increasingly valuable in the future.

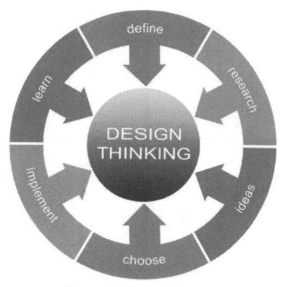

Figure 4.4. Design thinking.

CHAPTER 5

Final Notes

"Only half of what you hear is true. Learning is to discover that, and then to ignore the rest. "
- Pasi Sahlberg

Hopefully, you have been introduced to some new ideas about the potential of education in the future as you've read the previous chapters. As I mentioned earlier, this book is not meant to be all-encompassing, but rather an overview of some innovative technologies, like virtual reality and artificial intelligence, and the best practices of online e-learning.

However, there are many more technologies that will contribute to the future of education. In this final chapter, I wanted to bring two additional technologies to your attention, while also sharing some key examples from the Finnish educational system and some of the ways that other countries can learn from their example. As a native of Finland myself, I'm proud of the academic reforms that have been made there over the years and look forward to seeing others benefit from their educational models.

3-D Printing in Education

3-D printing is rapidly growing and becoming more popular in the education field as there is a full range of creative ways to use it in learning environments. Basically 3-D printing means that you can take any digital file and turn it into a three- dimensional physical product. This type of learning where students can create something tangible can be extremely interesting and rewarding, compared to just learning by watching images of something. Basically everything that used to be in text books, described by text and images, can be 3-D printed in the future, which will provide much more memorable experiences for students and increase motivation and commitment. For example, business students will be able to create a new product, and rather than just drawing a sketch of it on paper, they will be able to 3-D print it and have a real world example.

Using Blockchain Technology for Certificate Authentication

One of the most game-changing technologies that we will see over the course of the next few years is known as blockchain. As the name implies, it refers to a *block of chains* that is used to record transactions. Perhaps the most common example of blockchain technology comes from Bitcoin, which uses it to create a ledger in which Bitcoin transactions can be recorded.

Soon, blockchain technology will be used in the finance industry for everything from insurance and payments to banking and money transfers. It may also be used for voting records. Others will likely find additional creative uses for this technology.

Experts in technology are current working with blockchain concepts to see how they may be implemented in universities to track academic certifications and other information. In fact, Holberton School in San Francisco in the United States has already put out an announcement that they will use blockchain services to secure and authenticate all certificates. Blockchain is a unique and promising technology that can make transactions occur at a more rapid pace with better security control for users[14].

Learning From the Finnish Model of Education

Finland is one of the countries that is well-known for having innovative and effective school systems. With less homework and more emphasis on the individuality of students, this education system avoids the drawbacks of student competition and focuses resources on teacher training. To learn more about the Finnish educational system, I highly recommend reading the book *Finnish Lessons 2.0: What Can the World Learn from Educational Change in Finland?* by Pasi Sahlberg.

I would also recommend that you learn more about the HundrED project, which is an effort to gather 100 interviews with educational leaders and to explore 100 innovations within the Finnish education system. The results of this study will be available at no cost. To follow this project and to read more about it, visit *www.hundred.fi*

You can also learn more about the Finnish educational system from Satu Järvinen, who offers a great summary of the reasons why education is of such a high quality in Finland.

Expert opinion - - SATU JÄRVINEN

What other countries can learn from the Finnish education system is that each student learns in his or her own unique way, and therefore the focus of education should be to support the development and growth of every student, helping each one to reach their highest potential. The aim is to foster the unique strengths of every student, rather than to have a one-method-fits-all type of system.

In the Finnish education system, most of the schools and teachers see every child as a unique person with his or her own way of learning and understanding this world. The schools don't only teach subjects, they also teach how to examine phenomena in this world, to solve complex problems, to be creative, (painting, music, etc.), to be responsible for your actions ... all the skills needed for living a good life, really. The overall goal of the system is to develop good citizens who lead happy and prosperous lives. We cannot achieve this goal with traditional approaches to education.

For me, what is special about the Finnish education system is how it excels in building everything around having happy and healthy students with the knowledge, skills and competencies required to live just like in a fairytale: happily ever after. That, for me, is the big secret of Finnish education excellence.

- Satu Järvinen, Director of Education Services at Koulu Group

NOTES

Chapter 1:

1) Karla Gutierrez "Studies Confirm the Power of Visuals in eLearning" July 08, 2014, accessed September 13, 2016, *http://info.shiftelearning.com/blog/bid/350326/S tudies-Confirm-the-Power-of-Visuals-in-eLearning*

Chapter 2:

2) Ray Kurzweil "Don't fear artificial intelligence" December 30, 2014, accessed September 14, 2016 *http://www.kurzweilai.net/dont-fear-artificial-intelligence-by-ray-kurzweil*

3) Kevin Kelly, "The Inevitable : Understanding the 12 Technological Forces That Will Shape Our Future" June 7, 2016, accessed September 14, 2016

4) Jessica Conditt, "Tech's biggest names are working to regulate AI research" September 1, 2016, accessed September 14, 2016 *https://www.engadget.com/2016/09/01/facebook-google-microsoft-amazon-ibm-ai-panel/*

5) David J. Hill "AI Teaching Assistant Helped Students Online—and No One Knew the Difference". May 11, 2016, accessed September 14, 2016 *http://singularityhub.com/2016/05/11/ai-teaching-assistant-helped-students-online-and-no-one-knew-the-difference/*

6) Knewton website, "KNEWTON LAUNCHES FREE & OPEN ADAPTIVE LEARNING—FOR EVERYONE". August 26, 2015, accessed September 14, 2016 *https://www.knewton.com/resources/press/knewton-launches-free-open-adaptive-learning-for-everyone/*

7) Peter Stone, Rodney Brooks, Erik Brynjolfsson, Ryan Calo, Oren Etzioni, Greg Hager, Julia Hirschberg, Shivaram Kalyanakrishnan, Ece Kamar, Sarit Kraus, Kevin Leyton-Brown, David Parkes, William Press, AnnaLee Saxenian, Julie Shah, Milind Tambe, and Astro Teller. "Artificial Intelligence and Life in 2030." One Hundred Year Study on Artificial Intelligence: Report of the 2015-2016 Study Panel, Stanford University, Stanford, CA, September 2016. Accessed: September 14 2016. http://ai100.stanford.edu/2016-report.

Chapter 3:

8) Casey Sapp, "How Virtual Reality Can Close Learning Gaps in Your Classroom" September 7, 2015, accessed September 14, 2016 *https://www.edsurge.com/news/2015-09-07-how-virtual-reality-can-close-learning-gaps-in-your-classroom*

9) Mark Zuckerberg, "Live with developers and entrepreneurs in Lagos!" August 21, 2016, accessed September 14, 2016 *https://www.facebook.com/zuck/videos/vb.4/101 03071243629941/?type=2&theater*

10) Eric Johnson, " What are the differences among virtual, augmented and mixed reality?" July 13, 2016, accessed September 14, 2016 *http://www.recode.net/2015/7/27/11615046/wha ts-the-difference-between-virtual-augmented-and-mixed-reality*

11) James Mackie, "James Mackie puts it out there - the next technology megatrend" March 1, 2016, accessed September 14, 2016 *http://www.mackie.xyz/james-mackie-puts-it-out-there-the-next-technology-megatrend/*

Chapter 4:

12) Mydee Lasquite, "Storytelling: A Content Marketing Power Tool", August 26, 2015, accessed September 14, 2016 *http://blog.visme.co/storytelling-content-marketing/*

13) World Economic Forum, "The Future Of Jobs", January 18, 2016, accessed September 14, 2016 *https://www.weforum.org/reports/the-future-of-jobs*

Chaper 5:

14) Julien Barbier, "Using the blockchain to secure and authentify Holberton School certificates", October 21, 2015, accessed September 14, 2016 *https://blog.holbertonschool.com/using-the-blockchain-to-secure-and-authentify-holberton-school-certificates*

ABOUT THE AUTHOR

Lasse Rouhiainen

An international leading authority on video marketing and social media, Lasse Rouhiainen is an in-demand speaker and trainer for business schools and universities on how to maximize exposure on YouTube, Facebook, and how to implement social media marketing strategies. Lasse provides guidance and training for corporations, business schools and universities looking to benefit from the latest social media marketing trends and offers training in three different languages (English, Spanish and Finnish).

82640670R00055

Made in the USA
Middletown, DE
04 August 2018